WORLD OF
STEAM RAILWAYS

WORLD OF
STEAM RAILWAYS

by
Colin Garratt

SUNBURST BOOKS

CONTENTS

INTRODUCTION

It is with pleasure that I present this volume of pictures from my 25-year odyssey documenting the last Steam Locomotives of the World. The task began in 1969 when, fired with an ambition to create the kind of pictures contained within these covers, I abandoned a successful commercial career. Mounting the global expeditions was horrendously difficult, not least because the entire operation was a desperate race against time. Steam trains had already vanished from North America, Britain and parts of Europe as railway administrations across the world opted for more modern forms of traction. But the steam locomotive's all-consuming role in social and industrial history meant that it had to be documented; someone had to record the dying moments of so great a legend - not in a technical way, for that had been done adequately elsewhere - but in the workaday environment amid the diverse landscape of the world.

From the outset I tried to give priority either to countries in which steam was fast disappearing, or places where rare survivors lingered - and there were many 25 years ago; crane engines, tram engines, broad-gauge engines (7ft), Kitson Meyers, Compound Mallets, Shays, classic war engines, or simply centenarians which represented long vanished patterns of locomotive development. The task was made doubly difficult by the large areas of the world under hardline political regimes which rendered detailed and prolonged photography virtually impossible; Russia, China, Eastern Europe, Cuba, Mozambique and Angola being obvious examples. The situation has now eased in many of these areas, but steam has declined proportionately during the interim. Even China, which has opened up and to which I have made eight expeditions, is now down to four principal types on the standard gauge.

Many of the early expeditions were necessarily long: Latin America seven months; Europe and the Middle East five months; South-East Asia four months; Southern Africa three months; along with four Indian trips of several months duration.

The rate at which expeditions could be done was constantly blighted by the need to raise funds. I set a target of being overseas four months of each year, and fund raising during the remainder, principally from publishing books - 30 to date - and embarking on gruelling nationwide lecture tours and audio/visual presentations. At the end of several months of shows - from which I usually returned home during the early hours of the morning - almost total exhaustion would set in. Days later would be an expedition to the opposite end of the world where the climate and social conditions were radically different. However, the ability of the human constitution to adapt is virtually without limit, and sickness and fatigue which characterised all the early forays diminished as I adapted becoming ever more robust even in the most adverse circumstances. An average

6

working week during those first twenty years was well in excess of one hundred hours continuously. This had to be accepted if even the most modest progress was to be made.

I must not appear to give the impression of strife and arduous toil; it was, of course, immense fun and constantly stimulating. The adventures came tumbling one after another along with the joy and privilege of visiting lands of every conceivable climate, cultural background and political system, interfacing one to one at a grass roots level unseen and unimagined by the average tourist. I can also say with immense pride that, through all the experiences and vicissitudes, my faith in human nature and the human condition has been fortified, and this is a source of deep satisfaction.

The work continues apace although, parallel with the expeditions, is the need to digitise the most valuable images as the collection's real worth will only be realised in years to come.

The expeditions have also helped me to understand the essential rightness of railways as a form of transport. It is not just the steam locomotive which has died, but many railways too, as the mania for road transportation sweeps across the developing nations. This prompted me to form Milepost 92½, an audio/visual photographic service and picture library for the railway industry. Never has the need to promote railways been greater. In this respect the steam locomotive remains a living force, as it teaches us that the railway age was a totally viable and a civilised alternative to the hideous consequences of basing national economies on road transportation with industry, commercial centres, leisure amenities and residential complexes being wantonly placed away from rail connections. This has enabled right-leaning politicians to make the trite claim that the railway cannot sustain a modern society's needs.

So, the legacy of the first twenty-five years is a matchless collection of images and a production company which relates to the needs of the modern railway - the sequencing and design of this book being done at Milepost alongside corporate audio/visuals for the latest technical innovations. This is surely the perfect situation, the past being largely irrelevant if it teaches us nothing about today and tomorrow.

Turn the ensuing pages and enjoy the pictures; their like can never be repeated.

Colin Garratt
Newton Harcourt, Leicestershire
July, 1994

BRITAIN

The steam locomotive was arguably Britain's greatest technological gift to mankind. Its inception during the early years of the 19th century advanced the industrial revolution at a phenomenal rate. Before railways, growth and invention were stunted by the need for efficient transport. The railway age enabled all bonds to be broken; Britain became the workshop of the world and at the heart of that workshop lay the steam locomotive.

PAGES 8-13: Never will I forget the expedition to the Azores in 1981 in search of the world's last 7ft gauge engines. They were found covered in junk and debris in the harbour scrapyard at Ponta Delgada on the island of Sao Miguel. Until 1973 they had been employed to convey rocks and pre-cast concrete blocks from an inland quarry to the harbour for reinforcing the breakwater - as fast as the boulders were dropped into place the ferocious Atlantic storms would wash them out to sea.

Work began on clearing the site with the aid of six men, a 10-tonne crane, a fork-lift truck and a lorry; photography began the following day. The drama was well reported in the British media and on the morning of November 17th 1981 John Timpson, speaking on BBC Radio 4's "Today" programme, announced that a historic discovery had been made in the Azores. Many listeners regarded the report as a joke; the broad gauge had disappeared almost a century previously; the Azores had no railways and,

Britain's railways were developed piecemeal by private companies with the locomotives coming from outside firms, but once the operating companies joined together to form larger organisations they established their own works for overhauling and building. These company workshops caused places like Crewe, Doncaster, Derby and Swindon to become known as the "Railway Towns". Tens of thousands of locomotives were built from these and other towns - over seven thousand from Crewe alone - all for home use.

if they had, tiny islands whose average size is a mere twenty miles by eight miles - lost in the middle of the Atlantic - would be the last place to find a broad-gauge railway. As these pictures show the legend was real.

The works plate on page 8 reveals that one engine had been exported from the Falcon Works, Loughborough in 1888 as their number 165 - the Falcon being the right hand engine on pages 10-11.

The great export trade which developed as Britain took railways - and with them the industrial revolution - to many parts of the world continued to be conducted by private builders who in turn made cities like Manchester, Leeds, Newcastle and Glasgow famous world-wide.

The other locomotive bore no visible identification e.g. Works plates or numbers, but it is believed to be **from Black Hawthorn of Gateshead as their number 766 built sometime in the early 1880's.**

LEFT AND TOP RIGHT: Spain has long been noted as a haven of antiquities and as late as 1987, could still boast a 102-year-old metre-gauge Sharp Stewart 0-6-0T named El Esla. She came from the company's works on Great Bridgewater Street, Manchester before the firm moved to Glasgow. When this engine was exported from Liverpool docks, Queen Victoria had another 16 years to rule the British Empire.

ABOVE: Oil cans and grease gun on the footplate of El Esla.

**The characteristic 19th-century form of a Sharp
Stewart is well represented in these studies of El Esla.**

LEFT AND ABOVE: The Tharsis Sulphur and Copper Company in southern Spain was famous for its classic Scottish 'Pugs'. On the left is Dübs 0-4-0 saddle tank "Saucita" in company with derelict mine workings and defunct water column. Sister engine "Odiel" was Dübs number 231 of 1867.

BELOW: When Henry Dübs built his famous works in Glasgow's Queens Park he stamped the bricks with a diamond, and subsequently used the same shape for his builder's plates.

There were many occasions when the railway company's works were unable to produce locomotives quickly enough, and batches were commissioned from the private builders, but invariably to the railway company's design.

LEFT AND BELOW: These Scottish 'Pugs' are amongst the oldest and rarest locomotives to survive. Though out of use they are not preserved and thus liable to be broken up. "Odiel" (below) is 128 years old, but in spite of not having worked for some years is still complete and ostensibly operable. Their builder

Henry Dübs is one of the most famous of British locomotive manufacturers. Along with Sharp Stewart and Neilson his was one of Glasgow's big three foundries which amalgamated in 1903 to form the mighty North British, which became Europe's largest producer of locomotives.

PAGES 22-25: Pictures on this and the following spread depict the final moments of the world's last Kitson Meyer 0-6-6-0T as she ekes out her final gasps amid Chile's waterless Atacama Desert. The Kitson Meyers were an articulated predecessor of the more successful Garratt. The type was prolifically used on the Anglo Chilean Nitrate Company's railways bringing nitrate and gold from the desert to ports along the Pacific coast, a once vast and thriving industry which finally closed in 1970. At its height the industry employed enormous numbers of British personnel and foxes were imported into the desert in order for that most British of pursuits, fox-hunting, to be enjoyed.

The design, practice and development of the main line company's locomotives always exerted an influence on the products of the private builders who sent overseas engines almost identical with those running in the mother country - albeit scaled to different gauges - the premise being that what was good for Britain was good for the rest of the world too. Virtually no engines from Britain's main line railways were ever exported except as part of wartime operations. One would imagine that redundant engines from Britain would be pensioned off overseas for a further lease of life, especially towards the end of steam when thousands of locomotives - some almost new - were broken up; but it never happened.

On my arrival in 1979, the principal port of Taltal resembled a Nevada ghost town: dismantled buildings, abandoned jetties, derelict store sheds and rusted railway sidings. The wharves from which the nitrate was loaded on to the ships were partly diminished, though still decked with the skeletons of silent cranes. I found the scrapyard of the Kitson Meyer; pieces of plate frames, cylinders, boiler tubes, wheel fragments, tanks and chimneys. Amid the ruins of the old general offices lay a *Girls' Annual* of 1912. Here was full evidence of Britain at its peak of civilisation. This last working Kitson Meyer exploded in a geyser of steam seconds after these pictures were made and another fragment of locomotive evolution became extinct.

Britain ran relatively light and frequent trains; distances were short and the country highly populated. Throughout history, Britain's locomotives were generally smaller than in other parts of the developed world. Until the turn of the century nothing larger than a 4-4-0 or Atlantic was used for express passenger work, whilst freight operations were primarily in the hands of the ubiquitous inside cylinder 0-6-0's. This form of locomotive made its debut during the 1830s, and its final manifestation was over a century later with Bulleid's wartime Q1s for the Southern Railway.

PAGES 26-29: These, the last high-speed British Pacifics are seen ending their days unsung in far-away Bengal some twenty years after the last Pacific dropped its fire in the homeland. I made several expeditions to Bengal to document these thoroughbreds. Classified XC, they were exported to India during the 1920s/30s by the Vulcan Foundry at Newton-le-Willows in Lancashire and the legendary Clydeside shipbuilder William Beardmore of Dalmuir. Their overall design is highly reminiscent

The turn of the century saw the emergence of the 4-6-0 for passenger and 2-8-0 for the heaviest freight. By the 1920s the advent of the Pacific set the scene almost until the end of steam. The LMS 2-6-6-2 Garratts were a notable exception whilst ten-coupled power did not emerge in any numbers until the mid 1950s.

of Gresley's Pacifics - the very latest in style when the XCs were designed during the mid 1920s. The Indian engines, however, have two cylinders as opposed to Gresley's having three.

At the time these expeditions were made, the XCs had long since been demoted to working local passenger trains and pick up freights or even shunting.

For sheer good looks British locomotives were unbeatable; some were almost works of art, with beautiful proportions and rounded contours, all unsightly paraphernalia either being non-existent or carefully designed to be out of sight.

The last survivors were allocated to Calcutta (Howrah) and Burdwan which lies north of Calcutta on the main line to New Delhi. At Burdwan, an XC was diagrammed for the daily pick up turn to Bolpur as depicted on pages 26-27 whilst those on pages 28-29 show examples at Howra; on the left, alongside a traditional inside cylinder 0-6-0 and on the right, being coaled by a former East Indian Railways mobile steam crane which was built in Bedfordshire prior to the First World War.

Throughout the 19th century Britain had a virtual monopoly in the export of locomotives; after all, apart from the Empire, Britain was designing, financing, building and operating many world railways. But competition from America and Europe emerged during the early years of the 20th century. In some ways American locomotives - though not so superbly crafted as Britain's - were more suitable to world conditions with their wide fire boxes, bar frames and superior bearing surfaces.

It was vital that the final pictures of these last Greyhounds of British Steam should reflect their true thoroughbred lineage and this accounts for the three liveries of red, blue and green. I arranged for these colours to be painstakingly applied to the chosen locomotives and spent many unforgettable days riding with the Bolpur pick up. These magnificent engines were the last remaining link with a bygone age of passenger travel, when railways were railways as they never will be again.

The situation in Britain, with its abundance of high-calorific coal and well-engineered tracks, was quite different from developing areas of the world, and the ability of American engines to burn poor coal and cope with rough tracks was much appreciated by recipient administrations.

LEFT: There were three principal classes of Pacific in the Indian locomotive standardisation programme: XC (heavy), XB (intermediate), XC (light). Here, the last of the famous XBs is seen at Rajamundry ending its days on local passenger services around the Godavari delta in Andra Pradesh.

ABOVE LEFT AND RIGHT: The last XC to remain in service was number 22224; she ended her days specially decked in red livery. Here the engine is being coaled during the early hours at Burdwan in readiness for an 06.00 departure with the Bolpur pick up.

Britain's exports began to acquire foreign characteristics, especially American ones. Exported engines were often bigger than those used at home, with such wheel arrangements as 2-8-2, 2-10-2 and 4-8-2.

Sudan's railways were entirely British built and operated although in the last twenty years serious deterioration of the entire infrastructure and rolling stock has set in. This was so serious as to render the railway largely ineffective in alleviating the severe famines which occurred in the far south during the 1980s. Sudan has appealed to Britain for assistance, and much could be done given the will in the mother country but sadly, too much emphasis is placed on

Britain's great steam builders faced a further challenge when diesel and electric traction began to emerge onto the world scene. This time America had the lead; her railways were the first to dieselise on a massive scale; her building was geared up and America's diesel salesmen began globetrotting in earnest.

steam nostalgia and the attempt to recall bygone days, rather than putting energy into real railways upon which people's daily well being and lives depend.

ABOVE LEFT: A North British Pacific stares forlornly at a Hunslet 0-6-0T whilst on the right an oil-burning North British Mikado awaits its next turn of duty at Sennar junction.

This was also a time when railways in many parts of the world were under threat from roads; heavy trucking and private motor cars becoming much more prevalent than in the pre-war years.

PAGES 34-37: One of the last enclaves of steam traction in Britain was at Thomas Muir's scrap yard in Fife. It was host to a superb variety of Scottish-built industrial engines primarily from Andrew

Barclay of Kilmarnock, and ranging from diminutive outside cylinder 0-4-0STs to a heavy duty 0-6-0T with 18in diameter cylinders. The pride of the yard however was the rare centenarian Grant Ritchie.

0-4-0ST No.272 of 1894; she is seen at the top of page 34 confronting Andrew Barclay number 1069 of 1906. The pictures at the top of pages 35 and 37 reveal a tale of two Barclays. They show a pair of ex-NCB examples which were built together as works numbers 2261/2 respectively in 1949; they worked together on the Fifeshire coalfield and ended up side by side in Muir's dump. Above is Andrew Barclay 0-4-0ST No.1069 of 1906 with a 1950s MG Magnetti precariously perched on top.

PHOTOGRAPHS ON PAGES 38 AND 39: See caption on page 40.

The incredible Bagnalls of the Assam coal field are the subject of this and the following pages. The veterans were supplied to the Assam Railways and Trading Company, a British concern established to develop the wealth of upper Assam. The coalfield is located in the north-east corner of India some 25 miles from the Burmese border and about 100 from the Chinese border.

As a prelude to their operations, British pioneers sailed from Calcutta in Scottish-built paddle steamers, and plied their way up through the waterways of what is now Bangladesh, and on into the mighty Brahmaputra River to sail due eastwards towards China. They entered the dense inhospitable and leech-ridden jungles of Assam to develop thriving industries; tea gardens, timber and coal. It was inevitable that British Saddle Tanks should follow their enterprise. A century later these emblems of the British Raj soldier on as if they will never die.

TOP LEFT: Abandoned British locomotives of Ghana Railways in Accra shed yard where local people hold a a thriving, if illegal, market.

LOWER LEFT: Railway workers' houses in Sudan.

ABOVE: Nameplates from withdrawn Ghana Railways locomotives depicting former British officers, Tribes and a Slaving Fort.

RIGHT: British semaphore signals in Khartoum.

BELOW: A stationary boiler eerily simmers against one of the celebrated sunsets of the Nile.

LEFT: Ghana Railways' Vulcan Foundry 4-8-2 number 142 lies abandoned at Location Works.

BELOW: Ghana Railways Vulcan Foundry 4-8-2 number 266 "Techiman" on Accra shed.

RIGHT: The boiler from a wartime metre gauge McArthur 2-8-2 ALCO 70363 January 1943 supplying steam at a sawmill in Kumasi

LOWER RIGHT: Scrapyard remains of Ghana Railways 4-8-2 number 123 "Prince of Wales" built by Naysmyth Wilson of Patricroft, Manchester.

ABOVE: Ghana Railways' Sekondi Station in all its colonial magnificence with a brake compartment from the Midland Carriage and Wagon, Birmingham 1925. This site would have made a superb railway museum for Ghana had Britain not been inward-looking and parochial in her approach to preservation.

RIGHT: Ghana Railways 4-8-2 No.262 built by the Vulcan Foundry at Newton-le-Willows, Lancashire and adorned with a Giesl chimney - one of the last technical innovations designed to improve the conventional steam locomotive - lies amid the encroaching jungle at Location Works.

The fall-off in steam orders hit the British builders hard, and they were unable to adapt quickly enough to the new technologies. As the steam locomotive was dying on the main lines in the land of its birth, so vanished the famous builders who had made their cities famous from the jungles of Africa to the swamp lands of the Chacao; North British of Glasgow, Beyer Peacock of Manchester, Robert Stephenson and Hawthorn of Newcastle, and so many others who were destined to become guiding stars in the galaxy of industrial history.

The world's last all steam main line runs from the Paraguayan capital Asuncion 232 miles to Encarnation on the Argentinian border. Named F.C.Presidente Antonio Lopez, the railway is worked by wood-burning locomotives including Edwardian Moguls from North British of Glasgow, and a later version built at the Yorkshire Engine Company's Meadowhall Works, Sheffield in 1953.

The system was under British ownership until 1961, when it was nationalised and the fine Republica Paraguay emblems applied to the smokebox doors. The system is now in an appalling state of maintenance, the average speed over the 232-mile journey being 13 mph. Derailments locomotive failures, stops to refuel with logs, water shortages all take their toll.

Another amazing railway exists hundreds of miles to the north amid the wild Paraguayan Chacao. These systems were built to haul Quebracho logs from the interior to the river Paraguay, as the once prime source of tannin. After processing, the tannin was floated along the river to the Atlantic ocean at Buenos Aires.

The picture on page 49 shows Don Carlos, a Manning Wardle 2-8-2WT running as an 0-8-2.

ABOVE: One of the F.C. Presidente Antonio Lopez Edwardian Moguls eases up to a refuelling point. The logs, cut in lineside villages, are manually loaded onto the locomotive.

RIGHT: This 1950s variation of the original Edwardian Moguls from North British came from the Yorkshire Engine Company's Meadowhall Works Sheffield Two of these very LMS looking engines were built in 1953 and named 'Asuncion' and 'Encarnacion' respectively. There are many occasions when the constant flurry of fire from the chimneys of these Paraguayan woodburners sets fire to the log's in the engine's fender and also the wagons of the train as well.

And yet, years after the demise of these great foundries their products remain at work in far-flung corners of the world. Some of the veterans are over a century old and remain a living tribute to the skill and workmanship which went into their production. The long-dead hands which forged these classic machines may rest in peace safe in the knowledge that their hour constituted the greatest legend of all time.

The Rio Tinto mining system in southern Spain was a British-owned organisation which once operated a vast network of railways, sections of which were fully signalled. Workmen's passenger trains operated over the industrial lines, and the locomotive roster was as diverse as it was impressive, including Garratts. Following closure, steam locomotives were to be found abandoned at a number of sites although a representative selection had been set by for preservation. The picture to the left shows a gantry of semaphores presiding forlornly over a former trackbed.

LEFT AND RIGHT BELOW: During mining operations many years ago, a tunnel caved in and trapped Dübs 0-6-0T number 1515 of 1881. The veteran lay buried until being freed during the 1980s. The engine now stands on a ledge set in the side of a deep pit; retrieval is impossible, and the battered hulk of Rio Tinto Railway's number 50 is destined to lie in its rocky fastness for eternity. Reaching the engine for close-up photography was precarious, involving a difficult descent down the rock-face followed by a long hike over the boulder-strewn ledges on which the tracks once stood.

ABOVE: The Javan sugar-fields are one of the world's finest areas for steam traction. In many cases the lines radiate far out into the plantations with loading sidings at intermittent intervals. Temporary tracks are laid from the main lines and slewed in accordance with the cutting. Bullocks are used to convey the wagons along these stretches. The operation is typified in the above scene, with a Hunslet 0-4-2ST standing on the main line.

ABOVE: This twilight scene at Trangil Sugar Mill in Java depicts a locomotive which will go down in industrial history as being the last export from Britain. Of the tens of thousands of locomotives which have rolled on to the decks of British ships destined for all parts of the world, and carrying with them the spirit of the Industrial Revolution, this humble tank was the last. She was built by Hunslet of Leeds as their number 3902 in 1971, and is No.4 on the mill's roster. Originally she went to a Javan forestry railway, but was subsequently transferred to sugar-field service.

ABOVE: This late afternoon scene at Trangil shows their Hunslet 0-4-0ST No.4 at a loading siding alongside a rice paddy. The train is at Karanglegi Lor and the ever-curious village children inevitably flock to the camera. The boy's name is Iswanto; he is 13, and does not dream of the significance of the diminutive little tank engine which visits his local siding daily.

ABOVE: Early morning was a superb time at Karanglegi Lor, the low textured sunlight illuminating the engine's detail and throwing into superb relief the contours of Mount Muria behind. It will be seen that No. 4, in common with many engines in Java, is a Bagasse burner. This is the natural waste-product from the sugar-cane process packed into bales. Though low in calorific value, it is virtually cost-free and contributes much to the economy of operating the island's plantation railways.

PAGES **58-61:** The demise of Indian Railways' XC class Pacifics left the related XE 2-8-2s as arguably the most impressive British steam survivors. The X series were a set of standard designs prepared for India's 5ft 6in gauge lines during the 1920s and included Pacifics, Mikados, 0-8-0s and 0-4-2Ts.

As the XCs took their basic shape from Gresley's Pacifics the XEs followed the outline of Gresley's 2-8-2s of 1925. The XEs totalled 58 engines built by the Vulcan Foundry of Lancashire and Beardmore of Dalmuir between 1928 and 1930. They were the most powerful conventional locomotives India had, and for almost half a century hauled 2,500-tonne coal trains over the hill regions of Bengal.

Following World War Two a second batch of thirty five engines classified XE1 were supplied from Vulcan foundry, with detail differences, and these went to the Western and Southern Railways.

The last survivors were allocated to Asansol depot on the eastern coalfield in Bengal, where they ended their days on inter-colliery tripping and shunting duties. During the early 1980s they were despatched to Jamalpur works for scrapping, and by the middle of the decade were assumed to be extinct.

During this time I had access to the Eastern Railway's records in Calcutta and noticed that several XEs despatched to Jamalpur had not been broken up but, following purchase by various

industrial organisations - primarily power generators and cement companies - the engines were given a full overhaul and despatched to locations in various parts of India.

It was heartening to know that these last heavy British Mikados survived, and I determined to visit some of the locations. But the years rolled by until, in 1989, realising that it was now or never, I set off on a special XE expedition, much as I had done with the XCs a decade earlier.

It had been impossible to obtain reliable information on the status of the survivors if, in fact, they existed at all. The Indian authorities insisted that none would survive active; I felt differently, knowing the character and quality of British locomotives of that period. My instincts proved correct and four active examples were located, albeit in ailing condition.

The pictures on pages 58, 59 and 61 are the results of that expedition, along with one picture from Jamalpur Works (page 60) during the early 80s; she is No.22543 an Asansol engine built on the Clyde in 1930.

All pictures relate to the original batch, which are more pleasing aesthetically than the postwar series. I regard these pictures as especially valuable in revealing the final moments of one of the most fascinating phases of evolution in British locomotive history.

LEFT: The world's last steam railcar, built for Sudan like a battleship by The Clayton Wagon Company, Lincoln in 1928. She dates back to the time when Clayton built eleven almost identical railcars for the L.N.E.R. These bore the names of famous stagecoaches such as "Bang Up", "Chevy Chase", "Comet" and "Rapid". The steam railcar is in evolutionary terms the forerunner of the Diesel Multiple Unit as they not infrequently hauled a conventional trailing coach.

ABOVE: A Sudan Railways, blue-liveried Class 500 4-8-2 heads across the golden landscape with a mixed train. During my visit in 1982 only four of these magnificent locomotives were active, the remainder lying out of use awaiting spares, despite the locomotives being desperately needed for traffic. Forty-two of these magnificent engines were supplied to Sudan during the 1950s by North British of Glasgow. Although of 3ft 6in gauge they have a tractive effort of 35,940 pounds - almost identical with that of an L.M.S. Stanier 8F 2-8-0.

The former British Railway system in Sudan was built to 3ft 6in gauge. This once-superb railway has, over recent decades, been badly run down to the detriment of the nation. Some developing companies have been content to partially or completely abandon railways in favour of roads, but in Sudan the will fully exists to revitalise the network. Sudan's transport minister informed me personally "Don't forget us, let us have a dialogue with Britain upon how our railway can be helped and improved; with the railway skills inherent in Britain a new age for us could still dawn". Sadly, his plea was largely unheeded either by the British Conservative government or by the nation's millions of "railway enthusiasts".

Underscoring the legend is (left) a Hunslet 0-6-0T, one of the world's last "main line" shunting engines.

TOP LEFT: Late afternoon sunlight filters into an oil-begrimed locomotive shed in the Sudan in which Pacifics and Mikados reside. All Sudan Railway locomotives are oil burners - the country being devoid of coal.

LEFT LOWER: Applying oil to the motion of a North British built 500 Class 4-8-2.

TOP RIGHT: Maintenance is critical in Sudan - all workable engines desperately need to remain in traffic.

LOWER RIGHT: On shed at Sennar Junction: on the left is Pacific 4-6-2 number 246 North British 1940, in company with North British Mikado No.316 of 1950s vintage.

ABOVE: A tale of two engines on the Sudan Railway's line from Rabak to Khana, with Class 500 4-8-2 number 541 passing the wreck of sister engine number 514. Seven overturned and half-buried engines remain in Sudan, but with so many sister engines lying out of use for want of parts the retrieval of number 514 is somewhat academic.

RIGHT: Another drama on the Kosti to Khana line, as immaculately-trimmed blue-liveried Class 500 4-8-2 No.541 overtakes a plodding donkey cart on a typical dirt road. The combination of rail and local donkey carts is an affordable and highly workable system for moving freight in many developing nations as - in many cases - is the steam locomotive for its simplicity of maintenance, compared with the vagaries of infinitely more complex diesel and electrics.

Many of the world's steam survivors lie in graveyards or scrapyards, often partially dismembered. A handful are accident victims which still lie where they fell decades ago.

ABOVE: A sunrise scene dating back to the early 70s on the once vast Backworth colliery system north of the river Tyne. The engine - seen emerging from Fenwick colliery - is one of the famous Hunslet Austerity 0-6-0 STs. A classic war design totalling 484 engines built between 1943 and 1964. When the War Department disposed of their engines many went to collieries: they became a standard type on the National Coal Board who continued to order new examples from a variety of builders, and examples remained in coalfield service until the late 1980s, long after steam had finished on the main line. One batch did go to the L.N.E.R.; classified J94, the last of these disappeared during the 1960s. The Hunslet Austerities have the rare distinction of a type being built and withdrawn simultaneously.

RIGHT: The skies around Blaenavon at the head of the eastern valley in South Wales once glowed crimson from countless iron foundries as a revolution was born destined to change the face of the world. The world is girdled with Blaenavon iron, old-timers from the area will tell you. By the 1970s Blaenavon resembled a ghost town, only blackened structures and a heavy leaden atmosphere indicated that this was no ordinary place. One colliery lingered amid the blackened hillsides, and was host to a stud of Andrew Barclay 0-4-0STs, some named after the daughters of the General Manager during the Edwardian period. These veterans occasionally coloured Blaenavon's historic skies with fire, evoking memories of those halcyon days two centuries past.

LEFT AND BELOW: Hunslet Austerities predominate in these scenes as (left) one of Shilbottle Colliery's examples heads back to the pit-head with empties from the connection with British Rail. The picture below was taken as part of a BBC1 'Omnibus' documentary and shows the sidings at Cadley Hill colliery Derbyshire with the Drakelow Power Station looming in the background. This pit was the last to retain working steam and thus the great partnership of steam and coal - life blood of the Industrial Revolution.

RIGHT: A grime-stained Hunslet Austerity clanks a string of wagons back to the pit-head at Hafod rhy nys. The derelict structures of an industrial past dominate the foreground. A fall of snow transforms the blackened landscape into a shimmering texture; steam leaks from the ailing locomotive. But the depression remains, and the skies of South Wales remain perennially grey.

BELOW: An Andrew Barclay 0-4-0ST draws a rake of freshly lifted coals from the Pennyvenie mine in Ayrshire.

**Slag-tipping in Turkey featuring a Robert
Stephenson and Hawthorn 0-6-0ST and a superb
0-8-0T built by Bagnall of Stafford in 1937.**

The Buenos Aires Great Southern Railway, or BAGS as it was affectionately known, was a superb British railway which opened up vast areas of the fertile pampas to the south of Buenos Aires and conveyed millions of tonnes of beef and grain to the great Atlantic ports. These pictures reveal the decline of a once magnificent railway, as a former BAGS Class 11B 2-8-0 sits work weary in the decaying depot at Olavazzia, along with Class 15A 4-8-0s (below),

whilst the main line outside sees but a fraction of its former traffic.

Infinitely more hopeful is this 1973 scene from Witbank in the South African Transvaal, in which a Beyer Peacock 4-8-2 of World War One vintage contrasts with two American-built 4-8-2s of the 1920s.

TOP FAR LEFT: Indian Railways 0-6-0CT built by Manning Wardle of Leeds.
TOP LEFT, RIGHT: Dawn at Burdwan.

LOWER LEFT: Mixed train on Sudan Railways.
ABOVE: Indian Railways last surviving HSM Class.

ABOVE: A vigorous scene at Lucknow showing the colourful aspects of many Indian Railways locomotives. On the left is a traditional British inside-cylinder 0-6-0 - the trusty drudge and maid-of-all-work alongside an HPS Class 4-6-0 passenger engine.

RIGHT: Argentina's Buenos Aires and Great Southern Railway became the General Roca after nationalisation, following a policy of naming railways after leading generals. Here in the depot at Bia Blanca on the Atlantic coast is a former 5ft 6in gauge BAGS 0-6-0ST built at Kerr Stewart's California Works, Stoke-on-Trent in 1904.

BELOW: Mixed freight to Fray Bentos headed by Uruguayan State Railways' T Class 2-8-0 number139 *Engineer Pedro Magnou*. Uruguayan Railways echoed those of Britain in every detail, and this extremely handsome 2-8-0 has a distinctive 1920s Highland aura.

RIGHT: A former Buenos Aires and Great Southern Railway 11B Class 2-8-0 engages itself on yard shunting duties at Olavazzia. One hundred of these period engines worked the 5ft 6in gauge lines of the Argentinean pampas.

What was once good for Britain was good for the rest of the world too, and these inside-cylinder 0-6-0s represented the very essence of British locomotive traditions, and bore a striking resemblance to the Great Central Railway 'Pom Pom' J11s. Many inside-cylinder 0-6-0s were exported to India under the BESA standardisation programme of 1904.

The type was to be found all over the sub-continent, with examples passing to Pakistan and Bangladesh after partition. The examples here are seen at Malakwal Junction in the Pakistani Punjab - a cross-country town famous for British inside-cylinder 0-6-0s and inside-cylinder 4-4-0s, late Victorian Britain's definitive locomotive types.

The Garratt locomotive was one of the most important variations played on the conventional theme. Conceived by H.W.Garratt, the patent was adopted by Beyer Peacock of Manchester who built the vast majority of engines to this concept.

The Garratt's ultimate flowering was in Africa, where powerful engines were needed, but ones which were articulated and had light axle-loadings for working the tightly-curved and lightly-laid tracks. The Garratt fulfilled this role perfectly, and its

greatest single area of success was in Rhodesia, where the vast majority of the nation's steam fleet were of the Garratt type. At the huge sheds in Bulawayo up to fifty Garratts would be present, embracing five different classes ranging from 2-6-2 + 2-6-2 to 4-8-2 + 2-8-4s, and all from Beyer Peacock's works at Gorton in Manchester.

TOP LEFT: A North British built 4-8-2T delivers coal to a power station in South Africa's Transvaal.

LOWER LEFT : A heavy-duty saddle-tank built by Robert Stephenson and Hawthorn, Newcastle-upon-Tyne at Burnpur Iron and Steel works in Bengal.

TOP RIGHT : A Sharp Stewart 0-6-0ST hauls ingots between the mills at Cosim works near Sao Paulo Brazil.

LOWER RIGHT : The works plate of the Sharp Stewart 0-6-0ST above.

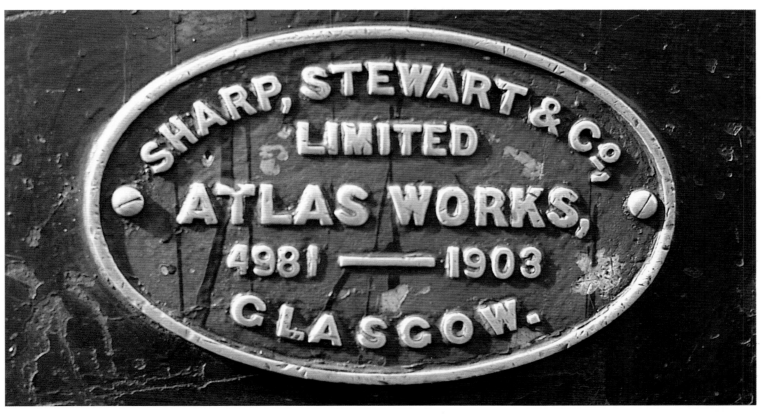

A miscellany showing the remarkable diversity of
Indian railway operation.

LEFT: One of the most handsome steam survivors in the world is this glorious Sharp Stewart 4-4-0 built in Springburn Glasgow in 1892 for Brazil's metre-gauge Mogiana Railway.

BELOW: This 5ft 6in gauge 2-6-0T is No. 9 on Indian Iron and Steel Corporation's Burnpur Works roster. She was built by Naysmyth Wilson at Patricroft in Manchester.

RIGHT: Mixed gauge at Hathua sugar mill in India with metre-gauge Sharp Stewart 0-4-0 *Mersey* of 1873 alongside a 2ft 6in gauge Baldwin 4-6-0T of World War One.

BELOW RIGHT : Oiling the motion of a former metre-gauge main-line 4-6-0 from Robert Stephensons at a sugar mill in Campos State, Brazil.

ABOVE: A further study showing the superb contours of the Sharp Stewart 4-4-0 of 1892. This engine was one of the high spots of my expedition to Latin America. She was one of several exported in 1892 for main-line passenger work and, although several derelict examples were located, we had almost given up hope of finding one active when this beauty was discovered at a sugar mill in Campos State. I spent the whole night polishing the engine with oily rags and bulling up the glorious brass dome and, as the engine slipped away to the plantation just before dawn, this picture caught her full glory.

RIGHT: A Beyer Peacock Mogul of 1899 struggles up a gradient on a Bazilian sugar plantation with a heavy train after tropical storms have turned the trackbeds into a muddy quagmire. Notice how the chimney top is eaten away - the result of years of fiery endeavour.

AMERICA

The story of the American steam locomotive is one of flamboyance. It evolved in three basic stages. The first is typified by the sensuous machines as personified in many classic Westerns; engines generous of loading gauge sporting enormous spark arresting balloon stack chimneys, cow catchers, brass bells, chime whistles and log stacked bogie tenders festooned with ornate lettering. These were the stuff of legend; the engines of the pioneering years.

BELOW: A Vulcan Ironworks 2-8-0 of October 1919 vintage works the Ramos line from Cuba's Simon Bolivar sugar mill. This superb system is built to the unusual gauge of 2 ft 7¾ in and is linked with the nearby Obdulio Morales mill.

RIGHT: This superb oil burning Baldwin 2-8-0 is depicted at Eduardo G. Lavandero sugar mill in Cuba. She was built in February 1920 as Baldwin number 52913.

Once the railway had opened up and developed the nation, industry and commerce boomed, so that heavier and faster trains were required. The classic 4-4-0's, Mogul 2-6-0's and Prairie 2-6-2's of the early years gave way to more powerful and rugged locomotives, so heralding the middle stage of development which lasted until the 1920s. This phase saw a huge variety of wheel arrangements and engines that were generally as powerful as any that would ever appear elsewhere in the world.

LEFT: An 0-4-0 Saddle Tank/Tank shunts the Carlos Manuel de Cespedes sugar mill yard. Built by Baldwin in 1916 she is an oil-burner the fuel being carried in the rectangular tanks on the running-plate - hence the designation Saddle Tank/Tank.

ABOVE: Baldwin 2-8-0 No.1661 of 1920 vintage belongs to Cuba's George Washington mill and is basking amid the sugar plantations at twilight. With yellow caboose at the ready the engine is preparing to take a loaded train to the mill.

The final phase was a period of steam superpower - The Greatest Show On Earth, as it was known. This culminated in the 6,000 horsepower 'Challengers', which could consume 18 tonnes of coal an hour, and the ultimate 4-8-8-4 'Big Boys' which had a grate area of 150 square feet and weighed 520 tonnes. Here was evolution's final fling and there was no greater contrast in locomotive history than Matthias Baldwin's *Old Ironsides* of 1831 and the 'Big Boys' of 1944.

LEFT: A delightful Mogul from H.K.Porter, America's leading industrial locomotive builder.
BELOW: A Baldwin built 2ft 6in gauge 2-8-0 of 1912 eases a loaded train along the scenic Arroyo Blanco line at Cuba's central Rafael Freyre mill.

TOP LEFT: A Baldwin 2-6-2T of 1904 lies out of use at the back of the shed at Cuba's Ruben Martinez Villena sugar mill.
TOP RIGHT: The famous flat crossing at Boris Luis in Cuba with classic American style signal box on stilts.

Today, only examples from the middle phase of development survive and all are exports. Not one steam locomotive remains in commercial service in North America. Having largely equipped the home railways by the turn of the century, America's locomotive builders began a massive export drive in order to keep their production lines rolling. Exports mirrored the characteristics of the Mother Country but invariably the engines were scaled down in size. Their rugged simple construction was well suited to the rough and tumble of the world at large. Most had two outside cylinders, bar frames, wide fire boxes, high running plates and in the later years a plethora of labour saving devices. American locomotive practice rapidly spread around the world either by direct export or as a result of design influences whereby other builders produced engines with American characteristics. The principal areas of influence were: Canada, Mexico, Central America, Cuba, Brazil, South Africa, Australia, Russia, China and, in the final years of steam building, India.

In addition, America produced a range of famous engines as allied aid for the First and Second World Wars. These were built in enormous numbers and to a variety of gauges. After the cessation of hostilities they were never returned to their homeland and became widespread around the world both through wartime operations and afterwards as disposals surplus to military requirements.

LEFT: A sunset forms an exciting backdrop to the fiery reflections from this Baldwin 2-8-0 as it awaits access to Cuba Railways main line from Carlos Manuel de Cespedes mill.

BELOW: 'A tale of two Alcos'. Derelict engines are to be found at many sites in Cuba and here an Alco Schenectady 2-8-0 of 1919 - complete with wooden buffer beam - rusts silently alongside an 0-6-0T built by Alco (Brooks Works) in 1916 for the United Railways of Havana.

ABOVE: 'Boiler explosion'. The remains of *Manuel Fajardo* - a martyr of the revolution. This 1916-built Baldwin 2-8-0 worked at Cuba's Obdulia Morales sugar mill. During the 1980s the engine's boiler burst. The driver, who was oiling the motion at the time, was literally blown to pieces - only his legs were found. The engine's bell, seen in the foreground, was recovered from a cane field a quarter of a mile away. The sound was described by local people as being like an aircraft passing through the sound barrier.

TOP RIGHT: On the overgrown formation of an old trackbed at Guillermo Moncada, Baldwin 2-8-0 No. 52914 of 1920 was found lying on its side with a derelict Porter Mogul in the background.

BOTTOM RIGHT: Front aspect of Baldwin 2-8-0, 52914 of 1920.

From 1905, the vast majority of America's locomotive building was undertaken by the "big three": Baldwin of Philadelphia, The American Locomotive Company (ALCO) of Schenectady in New York State and Lima of Ohio. These companies along with their subsidiaries built an amazing total of 180,000 locomotives; literally thousands of different classes being represented in this massive output.

ABOVE: Close-up of one of the many fine details used to embellish Cuba's stud of American veterans.

ABOVE: Slogans also appear like "Venceremos" - a rallying call for the revolution - "We shall overcome".

ABOVE: Cabside number style of one of Carlos Manuel de Cespede's 2-8-0's.

BELOW: Locomotive No.1385 belongs to the 2ft 6in gauge system at Rafael Freyre in Cuba's Holguin province.

ABOVE: An Alco works plate from a metre-gauge McArthur 2-8-2 in stationary boiler service in Ghana.

ABOVE: Typical Baldwin works plate from a 2ft 6in gauge Mogul of 1924.

ABOVE: A delightful detail from the cabside of a Baldwin 0-4-0 Saddle Tank at E.G.Lavandero sugar mill in Cuba.

ABOVE: Importing agents plate from a Henschel 2-4-0 tank of 1912.
BELOW: The Baldwin works plate from a 112-year-old Cuban 0-4-0 Saddle Tank.

ABOVE: H.K.Porter was America's premier builder of industrial locomotives and had the delightful practice of casting their name into the cylinder block.

ABOVE: This 2-8-0 is one of the most powerful locomotives in Cuba. It belongs to the Carlos Manuel de Cespedes sugar mill which runs - in common with many others - over the state railways' main lines as part of its duties in hauling cane from distant plantations. For main-line operations a caboose must always be used, and the delightful one shown here bears all the hallmarks of traditional American practice.

RIGHT: The cab interior of one of Cuba's sugar mill locomotives during steam-raising. All the island's locomotives are oil-burners as there are no indigenous reserves of coal. Many Cuban engines work heavy trains over long distances; crude low-grade oil has the necessary calorific value and is superior to cheaper alternatives such as Bagasse or wood.

Enclaves of this great locomotive legacy survive in ever dwindling numbers over forty years after steam disappeared from the home country. The finest examples are in Cuba, a nation which was under American semi-colonial rule before the 1959 revolution. After Fidel Castro came to power, relations with America were severed and hundreds of classic types became "frozen in time". Although most were built specifically for service in Cuba, some are actually ex-American railroads pensioned off to Cuba for a further lease of active life.

LEFT: One of the legendary Insular Lumber Company's 3-cylinder, 3-Truck, Shays trundles empty wagons back to the loading area on the Philippine island of Negros. The Shay's cylinders are set vertically and drive a horizontal crankshaft with pinions slotting into bevel gears on the wheels. Shays, though slow, could work over muddy tracks in logging areas and in situations where conventional engines would slip to a standstill. The brainchild of Ephraim Shay, a backwoods logging engineer, the type was adopted by Lima of Ohio and some three thousand were built.

ABOVE: The Insular Lumber Company's infamous 0-6-6-0 four cylinder compound Mallet number 7 eases onto the wooden trestle viaduct at Maaslud built in the classic Wild West manner during American colonial rule, with a load of teak destined for the coastal sawmill. Built by Baldwin in 1925, this locomotive had an awesome presence and was regarded by many workers as being a demon engine on account of the many accidents and deaths associated with it.

The humble survivors depicted on these pages are the direct descendants of those machines of the halcyon era when railways were opening up America and laying the foundation for the world's most powerful nation. Until the 1940s, the railway lay at the heart of America's infrastructure; a safe, co-ordinated, civilised and energy-efficient transport system.

ABOVE: **In the exchange sidings high in the mountains of Negros island, the last survivors of two epic variations on the conventional steam locomotive stand side by side spraying the tropical vegetation with fire. On the left is 4-cylinder compound 0-6-6-0 Mallet No.7, alongside Lima-built 3-truck Shay No.12 of 1907 vintage. Both are teak burners; the Shay has brought the logs to the exchange sidings and at dawn the Mallet will take them down to the coastal sawmill.**

RIGHT: **Lima 3 Truck Shay No.12 of 1907.**

America's rapid switch from steam to diesel during the 1950s coincided with the nation's love-affair with the car, and a road based economy developed with avid building of innumerable Freeways and Inter-State Highways. So extensive did road interests become that the decline of steam coincided with the decline of the railway itself, setting a precedent for other western countries to follow.

Today, a very different mood prevails in America. Many cities are choked with traffic and smog and a massive railway revival is under way. Billions of dollars are being invested in Light Rail and the creation of a national network of high speed intercity trains. This high-tech revolution, which will do so much to improve the quality of life in America, is based on the noble precepts laid down by those racy balloon-stacked machines of almost two centuries ago.

BELOW: The gradual reduction of the teak stands in the forest of Negros meant that little money was invested in Insular Lumber during its final years; the track became decrepit and locomotives badly run down. When the end finally came the world lost one of its most fascinating railways; it was the last logging railroad in the traditional American manner. The rasping syncopated rhythms of Mallet No.7 were silenced for ever and the engine confined to the graveyard where the inevitable vegetation rapidly took over.

RIGHT: Shay 12 and Mallet No.7 lie weed-strewn side by side, the ultimate contrast with the days when they stood side by side bathed in fire.

THIS PAGE AND OPPOSITE LOWER LEFT: On the plains of the Philippine island of Negros the red-liveried veterans of the Hawaii Philippine Company are hard at work. Officially known as 'Dragons' their 3ft 6in gauge locomotive roster is all from Baldwin's stable and consists primarily of 0-6-0 tender engines. There is also a pair of these 0-6-2 Saddle Tanks transferred to Negros from the Company's operations in Hawaii.

ABOVE: **One of Ma Ao Sugar Central's battered and hybridised relics far out in the canefields at the height of the crushing season.**

ABOVE: An 0-6-0 tank from Vulcan Iron Works lies derelict at the Bacolod Murcia Milling Company on Negros.
BELOW: Alco Mogul No.5 of 1924 at Ma Ao Sugar Central, with dry Bagasse in its sheeted tender.
RIGHT: The last Shay on Negros worked at Lopez Sugar Central - she is a 3-cylinder 3-truck beauty from Lima of Ohio in 1924.

LEFT: Shrouds of flaming Bagasse are flung into the air each time the locomotives move - despite their balloon-stacked chimneys which contain elements to reduce the emission of sparks.

RIGHT: During the early part of the sugar campaign on Negros some locomotives are converted to oil-firing until sufficient stocks of Bagasse are amassed. Here Hawaii Philippines Dragon No. 6 - in later blue livery - sports a stove pipe chimney for oil-burning and emits characteristic shrouds of black smoke.

BOTTOM: In contrast, Dragon No. 6 as a traditional Bagasse burner with balloon-stacked chimney restored.

One of the most famous war engines of all time was the U.S. Army Transportation Corp's S160 Class,

supplied as Aid to the Allies during World War Two. They conformed to the British loading gauge, and

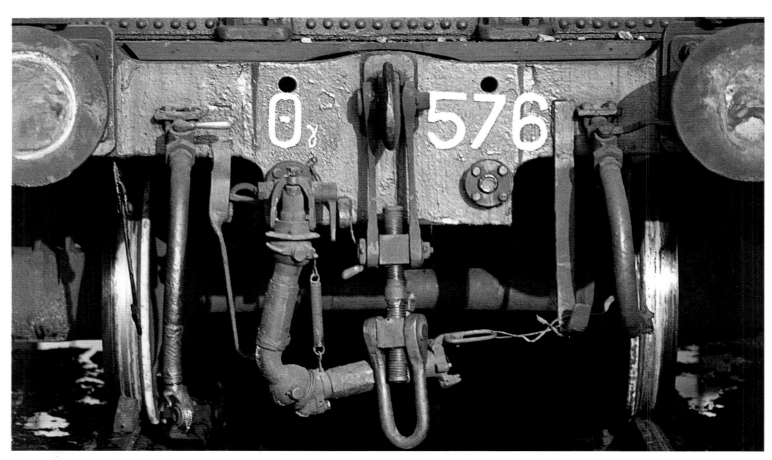

over 2,000 were built. The picture above shows an S160 alongside one of Britain's famous War Department 2-10-0s of 1943. These pictures commemorate the end of the S160s in Greece.

The post-war dispersal of S160's saw them scattered as far afield as China and North Korea, and a few survivors remain in both countries. These pictures show China's examples. Classified KD6 by China Railways they are confined to industrial service, working particularly in mining administrations.

LEFT AND ABOVE: The McArthurs are another famous design from World War Two. These were built to metre-gauge for operations in the Far East, India, Burma, Malaya, Thailand and Philippines during the crucial years 1942 to 1944. The picture on the left shows one of the Indian examples, while the picture above shows abandoned examples on the Greek Peloponnese.

RIGHT: The United States Army Transportation Corps 0-6-0 Tanks were another wartime classic and became as widespread as the S160's. They were built by Porter, Davenport and Vulcan. Survivors can be found in China, North Korea, the former Yugoslavia and Greece where this example was recorded.

ABOVE: 'Down at the Local Ironworks'. This 5ft 6in gauge balloon-stacked 0-6-2T was built by Baldwin for Brazil's main-line Paulista Railway. She was sold in 1944 for industrial service.

RIGHT: Contrast in Saddle Tanks as the ex-Paulista Railway Baldwin stands alongside a typical Scottish 'Pug' in the form of a Sharp Stewart 0-4-0ST of 1903 at the Cosim Steel Works near Sao Paulo, Brazil.

LEFT: A front view showing the remarkable form and gauge of this amazing American survivor.

RIGHT: A water column drips noisily at Tubarão
sheds on Brazil's metre-gauge Teresa Christina
Railway.

ABOVE: 'The Sunday Stoker', shovel in hand flits between an array of gurgling giants on the Teresa Christina Railway. His job is to tend the fires and top the boilers with water in readiness for the new week's workings. The engines are the world's last Texas type 2-10-4s. Built by Baldwin in 1940 these are American steam super-power scaled down for metre-gauge operation.

LEFT: Sunset at Tubarão shed on Brazil's metre-gauge coal carrying Teresa Christina Railway; on the left is a Baldwin Mikado alongside one of the system's 2-6-6-0 four-cylinder simple Mallets.

ABOVE AND BELOW: The Teresa Christina Railway had six of these handsome 4 cylinder compound 2-6-6-0 Mallets built by Baldwin between 1941 and 1949.

RIGHT: One of the Teresa Christina's most fascinating locomotives was this 1946-built Baldwin Mikado, nicknamed "Grimy Hog", originally built for Brazil's Centro Oeste network.

The building of India's railways was one of the greatest achievements of the British Raj and, until the Second World War, India's railways mirrored those of the mother country. India's final years of motive power development were characterised by the introduction of American designs, most notably the WP Pacifics and WG Mikados. The introduction of many war engines built to India's 5ft 6in gauge precipitated this, the country having versions of the S160 2-8-0's, along with the more numerous AWD and AWC Mikados, a larger version of which was built classified AWE. All have now vanished from main-line service but as recently as 1989 AWEs survived in coalfield service like the ones depicted on these pages working hopper trains in Madhya Pradesh.

RIGHT: American railroading of the 1890s is conjured up by operations on Brazil's 2ft 6in gauge system at Sao Joao del Rei with its stud of immaculately trimmed 4-4-0's, 4-6-0's and 2-8-0's. The system's oldest engine dates back to 1889, and its most recent to 1920.

LEFT AND BELOW: 'The Lavras Rose'. This delightful engine was the works shunter at Lavras in Minas Gerais state, Brazil. She was Baldwin's extra order No. 372 and was built in 1927. The engine is seen against a backdrop banana groves as it undertakes its workaday chores around the complex.

संजय

7124 NR

Pacific locomotives are rare today, almost all express passenger services having long since been dieselised or electrified. The most notable exception is India with its magnificent WP's. Though a standard design which worked the 5ft 6in gauge lines in all parts of the country, the WP's have attracted innumerable colour schemes and embellishments. Following Indian collaboration with Baldwin after World War Two, the first WP arrived from Philadelphia in 1947, making tremendous contrast with the traditionally styled British Pacifics.

WP's soon proved extremely reliable and capable of working heavy express and mail trains at speeds of 60 miles an hour. Building continued over a twenty-year period with engines coming from Canada, Poland, Austria and from India's Chittaranjan works in Bengal. The class totalled 755 engines and although many have been withdrawn, survivors are to be found in many parts of the country bringing India's steam age to a distinguished conclusion.

LEFT: A South African Railways "Big Bill" Class 15CA 4-8-2 passes traditional British semaphores on the Whitbank to Pretoria line, having been looped at Panpoort. Introduced during the 1920s, these American-built engines represented a watershed in South African motive power policy. Henceforth all new designs were American inspired and British influence came to an end.

BELOW: India was another country in which traditional British influence was superseded by American practice during the later years. India's main line steam fleet is now comprised of American-inspired types: WP WG WL YP and YG. Isolated examples of the classic British period survive on remote industrial lines. Even here, American influence is making its presence felt with large numbers of WGs being pensioned off into industry or surplus to main-line requirements. Here, one of the mighty AWE 2-8-2s - an American wartime version of the British XEs - shunts hoppers in Madhyr Pradesh.

ABOVE: One of South Africa's most famous photographic locations was on the main line north of Bloemfontein where from the side of a tall koppie the northbound trains could be seen climbing at 1 in 100 round this magnificent curve. Photographers of many nationalities would assemble here, especially in winter, as this hillside afforded a panoramic view of the surrounding veld. The line was remarkably busy, and on good days the exhaust from up to seven trains could be discerned approaching from the south. Here a Class 23 passes with an express for Kroonstad.

LEFT: This 2-4-0 is employed on tripping work around Usina Barcelos Sugar Mill in Brazil, much larger engines being needed for the heavy hauls over the steeply-graded lines from the plantations.

ABOVE: Most mills have a number of principal routes and at Usina Barcelos a stud of 2-8-0's were employed - like this veteran of 1894 caught bringing in the cane along the Pocogordo line.

These and the next two pages show the last survivors of a celebrated 60 cm (23½ in) design for military operations during World War One. With the war in Europe demanding huge numbers of Field Engines to move armaments and military supplies, Britain's locomotive builders were unable to produce sufficient engines quickly enough, much capacity being taken by the production of munitions. So, between March 1916 and April 1917 Baldwin produced 495 of these 4-6-0 tanks.

When the Great War ended in 1918, they were surplus to military requirements and it is believed that around fifty were sent to British India to work on the sugar plantations which were being developed at that time. Today, three quarters of a century later, survivors can still be found.

ABOVE: At Upper India sugar mill several of the World War One veterans are engaged amid the tranquillity of the plantations. Water supplies for the locomotives can be a source of difficulty, especially when detained out in the plantation for extended periods awaiting loading. At some mills a supplementary water tank is carried behind the engine. This scene shows a Baldwin 4-6-0 tank at the Jawan water tower at which it will thirstily replenish itself before covering the final section to the factory.

RIGHT: At Hathua Mill in Bihar the Baldwin War Engines work the 60cm gauge lines around the mill, whilst the connection to the Indian Railways main line is metre-gauge; the mixed-gauge track can be seen in the foreground. Ultimate contrast is provided at Hathua as the metre-gauge is worked by an 0-4-0 Sharp Stewart tender engine built in Manchester in 1873, and the sight of the two types side by side is unforgettable and captures the magic of steam in India.

EUROPE

The all-pervading British steam locomotive did not colonise mainland Europe. The area rapidly adopted the new industrial technologies, many originating there, and the wherewithal to build railways was rapidly acquired.

Mainland Europe's locomotive traditions fall into three principal divisions: German, French and Austrian. Germany was by far the most predominant: Prussian designs were very potent machines, enormous numbers being built, the P8 4-6-0s of 1906 and the G8 0-8-0s of 1912 totalling 3,800 and 4,000 locomotives respectively.

PAGES 152-154 (top left): The former republic of Yugoslavia was one of the last outposts of European steam. The country's railway history - like its political past - was diverse and this led to a rich variety of locomotive designs. The stud of former Serbian Railway's Class 20s which lingered on at Sîd to work lightly-laid cross country line to Begelina is an example. These delightful engines came from Borsig of Berlin a company noted for imitating British styling, and the 20s have a haunting North Staffordshire Railway aura.

Originally the type was destined for Turkey, and the first batch was en route in Serbia in 1912 when the Balkan War broke out. The Serbian army commandeered the engines and put them to work on their own railways; they fulfilled all expectations and eventually became a Serbian standard design.

TOP RIGHT: Poland's 600mm gauge forestry lines which lie in the north-eastern part of the country were host to the last Feldbahns, the German military field locomotives of World War One. These pictures were made in the primeval woodlands around Czazna Bialystock.

Following World War One, Germany's railways were unified and a standardisation programme was begun during the 1920s which included the O1 Pacifics and the 44 Class 3-cylinder 2-10-0s. In 1938 the Class 50 2-10-0 was introduced, which formed the basis for the Kriegslokomotiv (War Engine), of which over 6,000 were built to follow the German armies during their attempted conquest of the continent.

The Hooghly River is part of the Ganges delta, and flows into the Bay of Bengal - here, upstream from Calcutta, the Ludlow Jute Mills provide work for these Orenstein & Koppel built fireless engines.

ABOVE AND BELOW: Sunset over the Hooghly as a fireless takes raw materials over the jetty to the factory.

RIGHT: A Yugoslav State Railway Class 51 2-6-2T.

ABOVE: A Yugoslav State Railway Class 51 2-6-2T heads a mixed freight along the Karlovac to Sisak line.

BELOW: Derelict engines on the metre-gauge system on the Peloponnese in Greece.
RIGHT: A 19th-century 2-6-0T languishes amongst the wild flowers on the Peloponnese.

LEFT: A spider builds his web around the silent motion of an American-built S160 2-8-0.

BELOW: Golsdorf inspired 0-10-0s languish amid the huge locomotive dock at Thessaloniki.

FAR RIGHT: An overview of the Thessaloniki graveyard featuring American S160s, Austrian 0-10-0s and 2-10-0s.

ABOVE: Wild flowers abound amid the languishing giants of the Thessaloniki dump.

RIGHT: The wreck of Tithorea. A hulk I visited many times to capture the eerie atmosphere of this Austrian 2-10-0 abandoned in a lonely coppice.

ABOVE: The dead thistles of high summer echo the rusty tones of two Greek State Railways Z Class 2-6-0T on the Peloponese. Notice the old shovel in the middle distance and the dome cover from the right-hand engine.

LEFT: The symbol of a passing age in a Greek scrap yard.

RIGHT: The wreck of Tithorea in a different mood. The locomotive, the proud thistles, and even the grass have all died and the fallen lamp apes the hulk's battered form.

BELOW: The Finnish State Railway's TK3 Class 2-8-0s were known as 'Little Jumbos' and look superb, with their huge spark-arresting chimneys, running through the snowy-conifer dominated landscape. Descended from American practice most were wood-burners, although the example illustrated here is a coal burner with the standard chimney.

ABOVE: Prominent among Finland's last steam locomotives were the Class TR1 Mikados. Introduced during the 1930s, they survived until the 1970s, and amongst their last duties was working trains northwards from Rovanemi over the Arctic Circle into Lapland.

Finland's TV1 2-8-0s were known as 'Jumbos' and, at the time of my visit in 1972, the original total of 142 engines had dwindled to just a handful of survivors. Most were based at Kontiomäki in the north-east and I was fortunate to find this one diagrammed to collect a sand train from Hyrynsalmi close to the Russian border. The snow had drifted up to ten feet in the bank around this river bridge and, having reached my location with extreme difficulty. I stood shoulder deep in snow for three hours waiting for the Jumbo to pass.

During the inter-war period exports were made to Poland, Bulgaria, Yugoslavia and Turkey but the greatest distribution of German engines beyond their immediate borders was the result of two world wars which saw the spread of Prussian designs during the first, and Prussian and German standards during the second, either through wartime activity, or as part of the reparation packages Germany had to grant to aggrieved countries when the hostilities were over. As late as 1980 - 35 years after World War Two - examples of the Kriegslokomotiv remained at work in many East European countries.

Until very recent years Poland was one of the world's finest steam countries, certainly in terms of locomotives per square mile and in variety of types and gauges too. The main lines of Silesia were superb, with many long-distance trains hauled by the breathtakingly handsome PT47 2-8-2s which were by far the finest surviving examples of the Polish school of locomotive design.

Klodzko, where these pictures were taken, had an allocation of these TKT 48 2-8-2Ts which are Polish-designed general-purpose engines dating back to the **1950s. The type is interesting in having their smoke-deflectors placed either side of the chimney.**

Germany's most celebrated main-line builder was Henschel of Kassel, and in the field of narrow-gauge industrial locomotives Orenstein and Koppel with over 13,000 locomotives to their credit. Over half of these were exported for all kinds of industrial use worldwide. Orenstein and Koppel also produced the Fireless, which was one of the classic variations on the conventional steam locomotive.

LEFT AND BELOW: These pictures represent the fulfilment of a sixteen-year dream to return to Olloniegro colliery in Northern Spain to photograph the ancient Hartmann 0-8-0 of 1879 which worked there. I had seen the engine briefly in 1971 in heavy rain and cloud and vowed to return. When I did in 1987 the engine was derelict, but these pictures show the vintage characteristics of this extremely early 0-8-0.

RIGHT: A Polish State Railways Class PT47 2-8-2 heads away from Kamieniec with a cross country express from Klodzho to Katowice.

East Germany's narrow-gauge lines constitute one of the few highlights of steam traction in Europe. A number of lines survive, and these scenes on the 25-kilometre long metre-gauge Selketalbahn in the Harz Mountains show something of the magic - the principal power being these 0-4-4-0T Mallets which date back to the turn of the century. They are Germany's last working Mallets, and listening to the rhythms of their four cylinders as they pound through the woods and flower-strewn meadows of this delightful rural line is unforgettable.

Germany also achieved fame for her field and military railways developed during World War One. These gave rise to the ubiquitous Feldbahn 600mm gauge 0-8-0T. They came from 11 builders and totalled 3,000 examples. The post war dispersals of Feldbahns was widespread, and the last survivors only disappeared from the forests of North Eastern Poland in the mid 1980s.

BELOW: Another famous front-end in the form of this Golsdorf-designed 2-8-0 working as Yugoslav State Railway's 25 Class. She was caught in the woods near Ribnica working a Ljubljana to Kočevje freight during the early 1970s. Originally these engines were two-cylinder compounds.

ABOVE: The familiar contours of the famous Prussian G8 0-8-0, one of the worlds most numerous steam types. This immaculately-trimmed example was working on Turkish State Railways - allocated to Burdur, she was one of a small stud retained until the late 1980s for working local passenger trains.

German engines were - as one would expect - well-built and orderly in appearance, though more rugged than their British counterparts.

French design practice was highly individualistic and pursued compounding far more than any other nation. It is said that the French love of complexity is what adhered them to the principle. France was not a prolific exporter but, in common with Britain, exports went to areas under colonial rule such as Indo-China and French Equatorial Africa.

BELOW: German Kriegslokomotiv also featured in Turkey's latter-day steam roster, its light axle-load rendering it suitable for lightly laid routes such as this one radiating from Egridir. This Kriegslok was built at the height of World War Two by Maschinenbau und Bahnbedarf AG of Berlin in 1943.

ABOVE: A Slovenia picture made during many adventures with Tadei Bratè, the noted Yugoslav railway author. We chased the Austrian- and Hungarian-inspired designs across Slovenia over an endless succession of sunny days during the early 1970s. Here a former Yugoslav State Railway 17 Class of Hungarian origin heads a Sežana to Nova Gorica train.

Most French exports however were 'simples' in accordance with general world practice. France achieved a milestone in locomotive evolution by producing the Mallet, which first appeared as a four-cylinder compound in 1885. The Mallet principle was to divide the driving-wheels into two groups, the leading set articulated and the rear set fixed. However, the British Garratt concept superseded the Mallet in many parts of the world - especially in Africa, where French colonial influence might have been expected to give the Mallet a boost - so that its ultimate flowering was in America, where some of the world's largest locomotives were Mallets, albeit in 'simple' as opposed to 'compound' form.

ABOVE: A Prussian G8 attacks the steep climb away from the Turkish port of Izmia with a train for Buca. The trains climb away from Izmia, against an amazing backdrop of suburbs, with houses perched on every conceivable inch of the hillsides. The steady succession of trains provided a remarkable variety of motive-power ranging from Prussian G8 0-8-0s, G10 0-10-0s, Kriegsloks, German 2-10-2s, French 2-10-0s, Robert Stephenson 2-8-2s, and delightful 1912-vintage 2-8-0s from Humboldt of Paris.

Sadly, French locomotives were amongst the first to disappear and, by 1980, the only remnants were in Vietnam and Cambodia. Ironically, the last steam locomotives to work in France were rugged American Mikados. Classified 141R, 1,300 were supplied from America after World War Two to help make good the widespread devastation of the railway network.

ABOVE: What a magnificent engine the Yugoslav State Railway Class 18 4-6-2 was!

RIGHT: The unmistakable Golsdorf lineage of a Yugoslav State Railway Class 25 2-8-0.

ABOVE: The 2-4-0 is an early form of locomotive hardly ever found today, and this late example discovered at a Cuban sugar-mill was built by Henschel in 1907.

BELOW: Agent's plate from No.1207.
RIGHT: No. 1207 on shed. Notice the muddy substance plastered around the smokebox door to prevent air leaks.

Few steam-worked quarries remain, although they were once common. One exception in the post-Industrial Revolution era was this remarkable 600mm gauge system in central Uruguay, operated by a classic Orenstein and Koppel 0-4-0WT. The system - less than half-a-mile long - carried rock to the adjacent crushers in readiness for use as track ballast on the Uruguayan State Railway.

Europe's third principal category of locomotive development came from the Austro-Hungarian Empire which, prior to World War One, covered a huge part of Eastern Europe. The engines were principally the creation of Karl Golsdorf, Chief Mechanical Engineer of the Austrian State Railways from 1891 until his death in 1916. During his tenure of office Golsdorf designed 50 different classes, many of which were produced in large numbers, with building continuing for up to 25 years after his death.

Golsdorf was a great believer in compounding, although all his compounds were converted to simples during later years. Many of his classes were 2-8-0s and 0-10-0s with light axle loadings for the frail and tightly-curved trackwork abounding in Eastern Europe. They were thrilling machines to behold and, though festooned with external features and pipework, were strikingly handsome.

Originally a coal-burner, the engine has now been converted to oil-firing - the fuel, sufficient for one shift, being carried in the large barrel perched above the cab. It is said that this diminutive well-tank has worked at this site for half a century, and during that time created the enormous crater which forms the quarry.

ABOVE: A Syrian Railways Hartmann 2-8-0 lies in the works yard at Cadem in Damascus.

RIGHT: A Henschel 0-6-0WT brings stones from a Sumatran river-bed for crushing into track ballast.

For industries with a ready supply of high-pressure steam the fireless is arguably the most efficient and economical shunting unit. These engines are like a giant thermos flask on wheels, as one charge of steam from the factory boilers enables them to do much useful work around the yard before a re-charge is necessary. The only major disadvantage is if the engine runs out of steam at the opposite end of the line from the works boilers. This example at a Cuban sugar mill was built by Orenstein and Koppel in 1914 and is seen against the grey storm clouds which herald the beginning of the rains and the end of the sugar cane season.

The carving up of the great empire following World War One resulted in the emergence of Czechoslovakia, Poland, Rumania and Yugoslavia, all of which inherited Golsdorf's designs.

The upheavals of World War Two spread Austrian designs to further lands, with many examples surviving into the early 1980s, and appearing amongst the roster of the last steam locomotives in Greece.

BELOW: Turkish delight at the exchange sidings of the Catalagzi Colliery near Zonguldak on the Black Sea coast. On the left is a Turkish State Railways standard-gauge 0-6-0T supplied by Henschel during World War One, boiling up alongside one of the colliery's metre-gauge 0-6-0PTs built by Bagnall of Stafford during World War Two.

ABOVE: A brace of Orenstein and Koppel 0-6-0WTs bask in the sunlight at the Nsuta Manganese System in Ghana. They are Works nos. 10609/10 respectively, and were exported to Ghana in 1923.

RIGHT: Many of Argentina's railways were laid to 5ft 6in gauge, but the Belgrano Railway is a vast metre-gauge network. Here at the huge sheds in Santa Fé is 10A Class No.4606 - an oil-burning 2-6-2 built by Société Suisse in Switzerland in 1909 - raising steam. The veteran was built for the former French-owned Santa Fé Railway.

Many other European countries built their own locomotives. Italy was self-producing with a remarkable family of standard designs which dated back to 1905 when the State Railway was formed, but little exporting was done. Belgium and Holland were more prolific, as was Switzerland, whose designs stemmed from German and French practice.

ABOVE: Java's sugar mills hold a great diversity of multi coloured locomotives - most dating back to the early years of this century. Many are derelict and in the tropical conditions rapidly deteriorate, then becoming partly covered by the ever-encroaching vegetation. Here a forgotten and unsung little workhorse bearing no visible signs of its identity quietly rots, whilst in the background a raging sunset follows an afternoon of heavy rain.

Today the genuine working steam locomotive in Europe is on the verge of extinction; a few main-line operations continue in Poland with German-inspired designs, whilst narrow-gauge survivors can be found in the former German Democratic Republic and the forests of Rumania. Isolated industrials survive in many countries throughout the territory, and it is with these that the tradition will end.

ABOVE: There is no difficulty in identifying this superb veteran, as she is the world's last jackshaft-driven locomotive and, it is said, the finest hauling engine in Java - her geared drive being perfect for hauling heavy trains over wet and often muddy tracks. Named *Salak* after an extinct volcano she is an 0-8-0T built by Orenstein and Koppel in 1910.

ABOVE: Paraguay's all-steam international main line, which runs from the capital Asunción to Encarnación on the Argentinian border passes through the sugar-growing area around Tebicuary where a network of narrow-gauge lines once operated. Sadly, in common with many such systems, rail operations have now been replaced by trucking. The connection to the main line was worked by a standard-gauge Borsig built steam tram of 1910, pensioned off from the municipality of Buenos Aires to end its days in neighbouring Paraguay. Other engines silenced by the closure are

The situation is a little happier on the world front - the brightest spot being Indonesia, the islands of Java and Sumatra having a plethora of designs to work the narrow-gauge railways of the sugar and palm-oil industries. Some of these veterans were built in Holland (the territory being the former Dutch East Indies) but most are of German origin from Orenstein and Koppel. The Indonesian enclave is to European steam what Cuba is to American.

these two German well-tanks sitting forlornly in the former depot yards. This fiery engine (lower right) was the cause of my being arrested by the Syrian military. I had made the picture on the border with Jordan - the engine having worked in with an international train from Damascus. I was not aware that a major movement of military vehicles had taken place in the area, and it was reported that the foreigner with the camera had photographed these. It was a sheer miracle to have got this picture out of the country. Its loss would have been tragic as it shows a rare Borsig 2-8-0 built in 1914 during that German builder's 'English phase'.

ABOVE: Tebicuary's Borsig steam tram trundles along the metals of the international main line from Asunción to Encarnación, having delivered wagons of raw sugar to the main-line connection. This engine was almost certainly the last survivor of this form of locomotive which evolved for on-street running in areas where people and vehicles had equal right of access - such as docks. Steam trams found particular favour in Holland, and consequently in Java - once part of the Dutch East Indies.

RIGHT: The tannin industry of the Paraguayan Chacao resounds to the bark of vintage locomotives as they haul the mighty Quibracho logs from the forests. No train needed a whistle at night as the engines threw shrouds of crimson embers a hundred feet into the air, and could be seen approaching from distances of many miles. This engine, named *Lorita* is believed to have been the first locomotive on the Paraguayan Chacao having come from Arthur Koppel in Berlin in 1898.

FOLLOWING PAGES: Firethrowers also perform spectacularly in Java, when the Bagasse-burners throw half the contents of their fireboxes out of their chimneys.

'Bringing in the cane by night' was a theme I first explored in Java in 1974. The original picture depicted two yellow engines bathed in fire at Pesantren Mill. This return to the theme in 1989 has produced a tighter and more dramatic picture. On the left is No. 217, one of Pesantren's four-cylinder compound 0-4-0 Mallets along with 0-8-0T No.8 *Dieng*.

RIGHT: One of the most fascinating engines found on my second Javan expedition was this Orenstein and Koppel 0-4-2T of 1907. The barrels which adorn many locomotives in Java often contain sand, which is liberally sprayed onto the rails for adhesion following frequent rainy spells.

BELOW: It is a wonderful experience to ride out from the sugar-mills with the empty trains, drop the wagons at intermittent local sidings and return, progressively collecting a full train of loaded wagons. Sometimes the trips can take ten hours, but the time passes quickly sitting on the piles of bagasse in the engine's tender, eating succulent sugar-cane and enjoying the beauty and tranquillity of the plantations. One such trip was with *Banteng*, an Orenstein and Koppel 0-8-0T of 1912.

RIGHT: Over the last two decades steam activity has declined greatly on the Javan sugar-fields, and many of the engines working today are confined to yard shunting around the mill. Java has over 50 sugar factories, many in the eastern part of the island. Some engines are named - many after volcanoes, for which Java is famous.

Almost all Javan locomotives have spark-arresting
chimneys embracing an amazing diversity of shapes.

ABOVE: A shed scene at Comal Baru in Java featuring two Orenstein and Koppel locomotives built side-by-side in Germany in 1921 as works numbers 9297/8 respectively. Despite moving to various locations around Java during the intervening years they are seen here still together in 1989, almost seventy years after being built.

RIGHT: Another veteran to visit the ornate depot at Comal Baru was this amazing Orenstein and Koppel 0-4-2T of 1907. The two huge barrels signify that she is an oil-burner, whilst another mark of distinction is her use of Joy valve gear.

Amid the diversity of steam classes and liveries on Java is a wonderful range of nameplates, number plates, works plates, agent's plates and lining-out styles.

ABOVE: The name plate of *Dieng*, an Orenstein and Koppel 0-8-0T with Klimlinder axles. She is Works no. 6943 of 1913.

LEFT AND BELOW:
Builders' plates from Schwartzkopf and Orenstein and Koppel.

ABOVE: William H Müller agents plate from a 1926-built Henschel engine.

BELOW: The ornate nameplate of *Max*, a sprightly Orenstein and Koppel 0-6-0T of 1923.

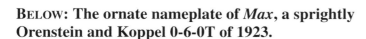

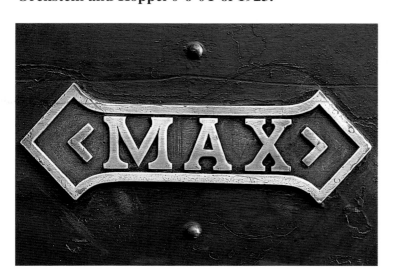

ABOVE: One of the many applied number styles.

ABOVE: The 2-4-0 was one of Java's earliest forms of passenger engine. This Manchester-built veteran of 1885 contrasts with the later German 4-4-0 opposite.

RIGHT: Until the late 1970s Java had a fascinating locomotive roster on the 3ft 6in gauge lines of the P.J.K.A. - Indonesian State Railways. Together with the sugar-factories this produced an exciting total of over 1,000 engines - some a century old - of at least 150 different types. Few countries could offer diversity on the scale of Java's. This main-line scene depicts a P.J.K.A. Class B51 two cylinder compound 4-4-0 built at the beginning of the century, and bearing more than a hint of Prussian ancestry. In the background is a Class CC27 4-6-4T.

CHINA

China's early locomotives were imported, but almost all the examples running today were built in China, though heavily influenced by American practice. This influence derived from American imports to China and through Japan, America having equipped that country's railways early in the 20th century. When the Japanese occupied the Chinese industrial heartland of Manchuria during the 1930s, American-styled locomotives were built for China in Japan - and also in Chinese works under Japanese control.

The expulsion of the Japanese, and subsequent founding of the People's Republic of China in 1949, led to a technical liaison with Russia and that country's practices made its mark, but again the American tradition predominated as a result of America supplying Russia with locomotives over many years.

LOWER LEFT: A poster from Datong locomotive works extolling workers to read the Little Red Book of Safety.

LOWER RIGHT: Incentive schemes and slogans are an every day part of industrial life in China - as they were when Britain was at its industrial height. The picture here, again from Datong works, relates to productivity.

RIGHT: The outer firebox shell of a JS receives careful attention from a welder - many of whom are female - in the boiler shop at Datong.

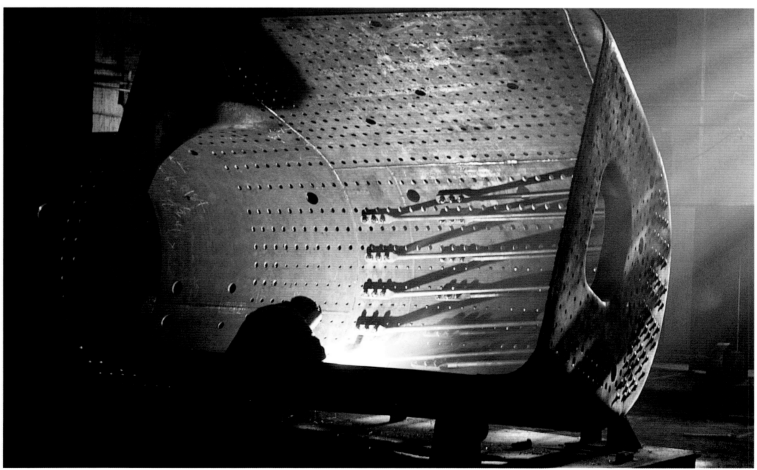

RIGHT: The sand for the castings at Datong Works is dried by flaming jets of coal-gas manufactured on site. Here a bleeder pipe burns off surplus gas in the casting shop.

BELOW AND TOP RIGHT: The steel tyres for the QJ's driving wheels are staked in position and spun at high velocity amid flaming jets of coal gas. The hot tyres are then shrunk on to the wheels.

LEFT: Smouldering castings from QJ Class wheels lie on the sandy floor at Datong Works.

Assembling a mighty QJ Class 2-10-2 in the erecting
shop at Datong Works, which is located in the north
of Shanxi Province on the border with inner
Mongolia. Datong produced over 4,000 of these
standard QJs, in addition to numerous JS 2-8-2s.

At the time of my first visit during the winter of 1983/4 the works were producing one complete locomotive every day. Over a twenty-five year period Datong built more than half the total of locomotives produced by Crewe in more than a century.

It was a great privilege to have visited Datong Works so many times during the 1980s when steam building was in full fling. This was over ten years after steam had vanished from Britain and twenty-five years after Britain's last steam locomotives had been built. Never in my wildest imagination did I dream of ever seeing steam locomotives being built again.

One of the most fascinating parts of Datong Works was the steam testing shed located far away from the deafening cacophony of heavy drilling and the ghostly pattern of welders' torches. Inside its gloomy portals the giant engines decked in their flamingo-coloured works undercoat were given the first breath of animation, to stand simmering gently for twenty four hours with gangs of blue-coated engineers periodically swarming all over them. Assuming that all was well, engines would go for test running, Datong having a separate high-speed track several miles long and this was used for putting new engines through their paces. The locomotives were run 'light engine' at full throttle reaching speeds of up to 60 mph.

China has never been an exporter of steam locomotives although in recent years she has expressed a willingness to supply any potential market.

The reason for China's inclusion here as an identifiable segment of world locomotive development, is based primarily on sheer numbers and the country's leading status in surviving world steam. China has by far the greatest number of active locomotives estimated at almost 10,000. There are now more working steam locomotives in China than in the rest of the world put together.

ABOVE: Filling a casting with liquid steel.

BELOW: Rough castings of locomotive wheels prior to machining at Tangshan.

ABOVE: Datong and Tangshan Works did not undertake overhauls. These are conducted at separate works throughout China.

BELOW: Smouldering castings for SY Class 2-8-2s at Tangshan.

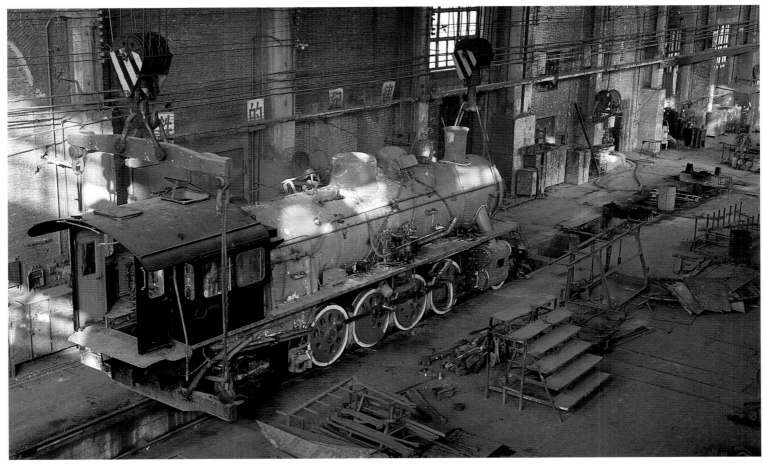

Tangshan Works is the home of the SY Class 2-8-2 Industrial Mikado. Over 1,500 are in service and building continued into the 1990s - the picture lower left showing a newly completed SY in the erecting shop being made on New Years Day 1992. During an earlier visit I watched an SY grow from its frame with the consequent fitting of cylinders, boiler and cab. The engine became a mass of welders' flashes until a set of wheels were placed in Mikado formation, the engine lifted by two overhead cranes and the wheels rolled into place.

Equally fascinating is the incredible degree of standardisation achieved with only 4 basic types in service. Two principal factors have enabled this to happen; firstly, the People's Republic adopted a communist system under which national planning was co-ordinated and dominated by central government and secondly, the railway came late to China; many important lines were not built until after 1949 and indeed some are in the process of being built today.

China has very few engines over 50 years old and the four principal classes in operation are: The JF 2-8-2; JS 2-8-2; QJ 2-10-2 and SY 2-8-2.

ABOVE AND TOP RIGHT: Changchun Locomotive Works is one of China's largest, and primarily overhauls QJ and JS Classes. The works employs 5,000 people and out-shops some 300 locomotives each year. The works target is to out-shop an engine within an amazing 20 days of its arrival, the operation being grouped into three principal phases: frame, wheels and boiler.

Certainly in Changchun - as in most Chinese works - one senses an atmosphere of unstoppability and I will never forget the words of one official who said to me in perfect English "Our workmen move like Charlie Chaplin did in your old movies".

BOTTOM RIGHT: Machine tools at Tangshan Works.

The JF is a classic American Mikado of the kind found on many American railroads during the early years of the century. They were built in Japan and China during the occupation. After liberation, JFs continued to be supplied from Japan, presumably as war reparations. Building continued in China until as late as 1958, when the first JS 2-8-2 was introduced from Dalian Works. The JS is a direct derivative of the JF, having virtually identical frames and cylinders. The boiler however incorporates Russian influences, with a Worthington feed water heater and large wind shields.

RIGHT: Named locomotives are rare in China but the 'Pride of Harbin' was QJ Class 2-10-2 No. 2470 *Zhou De*, the marshal who led the Red Army from 1927, and throughout the revolution of 1949, when he was second only to Mao himself.

BELOW AND FAR TOP RIGHT: Frenzied activity on the preparation pits at the mighty steam depot in Harbin with sand hoppers, ash disposal and watering facilities.

FAR BOTTOM RIGHT: The crew of a QJ at Changchun Shed.

China's most numerous locomotive is the QJ, of which some 4,500 were built from their inception in 1957 until the late 1980s. Six Chinese works produced the QJ - which was descended from the Soviet LV Class - but from the mid 60s production was concentrated at Datong. These mechanically-stoked giants have a 70-square-foot grate area and are capable of lifting 3,000-tonne trains. They were built with relatively few modifications over a thirty year period and appeared in most parts of the country. Some engines have large 12-wheeled tenders designed for service in dry areas. QJs frequently double-head - or occasionally triple-head - on major routes, the Chinese regarding the benefits of standardisation as being more economical than producing a larger design more related to the loads of today.

BELOW: Standardisation in China has reached an unprecedented level, but monotony is relieved by an almost limitless range of adornments of every conceivable colour. Some are merely decorative, but many of the more flamboyant displays relate to the engines' regular crews having achieved efficiency targets in such matters as fuel consumption and punctuality.

ABOVE: A winter scene at Shenyang. This town formally known as Mukden is set in China's industrial heartland of Manchuria. Apart from heavy manufacturing it is an important railway junction where the line northwards from Beijing joins that from Dalien on the Yellow Sea coast. Until very recently Shenyang Depot had an allocation of well over 100 locomotives, but the intensive dieselisation policy now being pursued by China Railways has decimated this. However, as this 1992 picture shows, the sheds are still worth a visit as is the railway museum set immediately alongside where many famous designs of the past are awaiting restoration.

The QJs are by far the most numerous steam type left in world service and are one of the classic designs in locomotive history. They have the rare distinction of being built and withdrawn simultaneously - some of the older examples being scrapped before the Class was completed. A handful have gravitated into industrial service.

ABOVE LEFT: One locomotive which has been restored to main line order at Shenyang is this SL7 Pacific. A classic from the streamlined era of the 1930s and one of the engines which worked the Asia high-speed expresses between Dalien and Shenyang. The SL7's design is similar to the New York Central's K5 Pacifics on the famous Mercury Express. It is perhaps not surprising that today's diesel-hauled services between Dalien and Shenyang are slower as well as less comfortable.

ABOVE RIGHT: This engine is a perfect example of the delightful variations the Chinese play on their basic designs. The engine is an industrial SY Class 2-8-2 No. 0964. Usually SYs are black and run without embellishments, wind shields or chimney casing. She was caught basking in the sun in Tangshan Colliery yard whilst taking a breather between shunting duties.

RIGHT: One of the most exotic railway photographic locations left on earth is on the climb northwards from Nanchan on the line to Yichun. The dramas during winter have to be seen to be believed, as the banked trains toil up the steep grades amid temperatures as low as minus 30 degrees centigrade. This section is also interesting as being one of the last places on earth where main-line steam trains are regularly banked.

RIGHT: Another fascinating variation in the form of a JS Class 2-8-2. This one is shorn of its usual accoutrements of wind shields, front number-plate cover and chimney casing. Once these Russian influences are removed the engine's pure American ancestry is evident.

BELOW: An industrial SY 2-8-2 under repair at Changchun Shed.

FAR RIGHT: This rare survivor at the Anshan Iron and Steel Works is one of the famous United States Army Transportation Corps 0-6-0Ts from World War Two. Classified XK2 by the Chinese, several of these American war engines survive for operating areas of the works with restricted clearances.

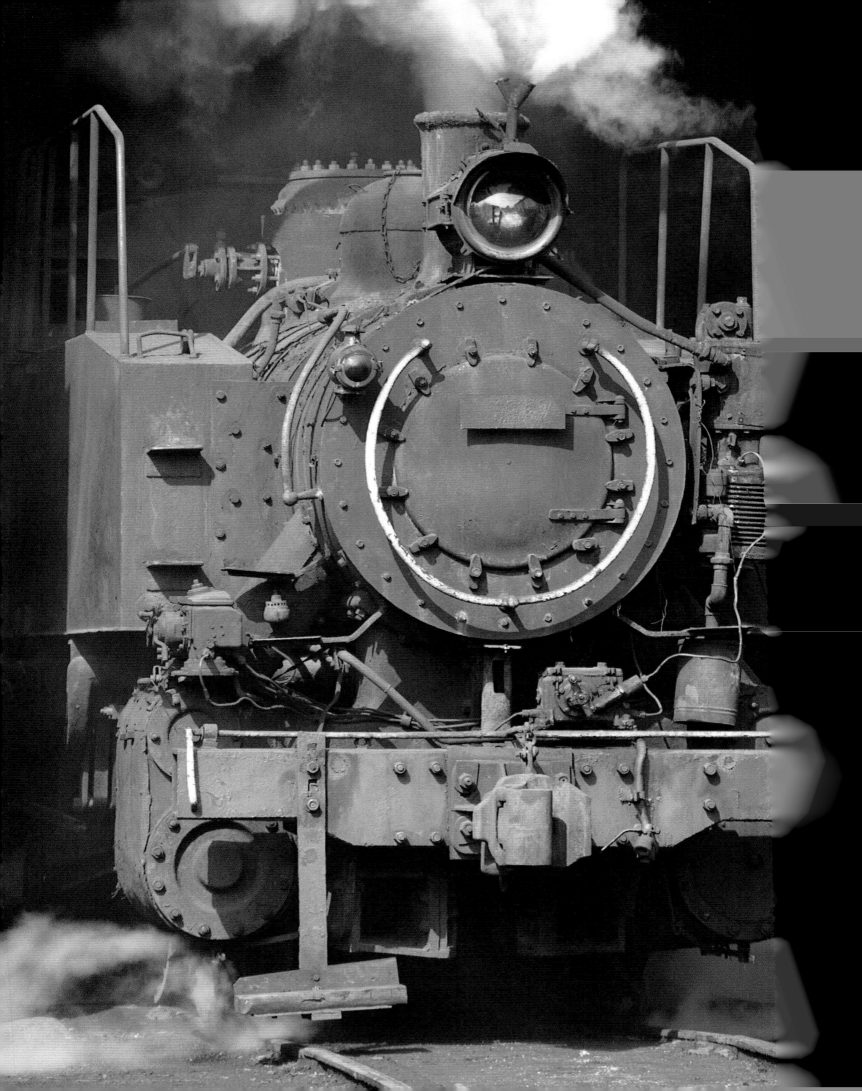

These three pictures were taken amid the sunlight, smoke and shadow of the steam shed at Anshan Iron and Steel Works. The allocation is predominantly SYs but YJ and PL2 Prairies and the occasional industrial JF and XK2 0-6-0T also appear. The depot undertakes light repairs, often whilst the engine remains in steam. The pictures here illustrate the diversity.

ABOVE: Two SYs bask amid the sooty magic.

RIGHT: A YJ Class 2-6-2 from the blast-furnace area receives minor attention from the acetylene cutter whilst (far right) one of the few main-line JF Mikados which have passed into industrial service.

ABOVE: A QJ 2-10-2 crosses the river at Fushun with a rake of oil wagons on Thursday 5th January 1984. Fushun is China's coal capital, and valuable amounts of oil are manufactured from coal. Normally the river would be frozen solid, but an industrial discharge has partially melted the ice.

TOP RIGHT: The main line from Harbin to Changchun was one of the world's busiest steam routes until its almost complete dieselisation during the late 1980s. Here in happier times is a QJ-hauled freight at Wang Gang south of Harbin.

LOWER RIGHT: Another line which on busy days saw steam trains passing every few minutes was the Shenyang to Dalien, and this location south of Anshan with Saddle Mountain in the background was a particular favourite.

China's other steam type is the SY 2-8-2. These are believed to be descended from the JF6 Class, which in turn is a descendent of an ALCO Mikado supplied to Korea. Built for industrial service some 1,500 SYs are at work, and isolated examples were still being turned out from Tangshan works well into the 1990s, giving them the distinction of being the last steam locomotives to be built.

Until 1990, two classes of Pacific were included in China's locomotive roster, but these have now disappeared, the vast majority of the nation's passenger services being in the hands of diesel or electric traction.

ABOVE AND RIGHT: A QJ Class 2-10-2 makes a laboured start from Sankong Yard in Harbin amid temperatures of minus 20 degrees centigrade.

BELOW: A Yichun-bound passenger train, having topped the summit from Nancha, heads across the wintry plain towards Liu Shu.

TOP LEFT: A QJ 2-10-2 bursts away from Harbin with a southbound freight along the main line through Manchuria.

LEFT: A JF 2-8-2 marshals a permanent way train in the huge open-cast pit at Zalainoer near Manzhouli in February 1987.

RIGHT: Sangkong Bridge in Harbin was arguably the greatest train watching place in the world. It overlooked the vast marshalling-yards, where a dozen steam locomotives would be visible at any one time, amid a sea of wagons which extended as far as the eye could see. Both the northbound and southbound sides of the yard were hump-shunted which until the late 1980s was performed by JF 2-8-2s.

Anshan is China's iron and steel capital, with all the
atmosphere of the Industrial Revolution.

Anshan Iron and Steel Works produces an unbelievable 13.85 million tonnes of iron and steel each year. The site comprises sixty plants, including ten blast furnaces, three steel mills, a sinter plant, coking plant, twenty rolling mills, two power-stations a refractory and mechanical repair shops. Ninety percent of the ore is locally mined, whilst coal comes by main-line railway from nearby Fushun. The entire Anshan operation employs one quarter of a million people.

The railway covers the entire operation and there are fifteen "main lines" from which branches diverge. During the late 1980s the total locomotive allocation was around two hundred consisting of steam, diesel and electric - the latter being used primarily on the famous Circle Railway along which the ore is brought from the outlying mines.

Every visitor to Anshan will have his favourite activity, and here are some of the possibilities: ABOVE: The XK2 in a quiet corner of the works.

BELOW: Tipping molten waste down the slag bank. RIGHT: Drawing the ladles of liquid iron from the blast furnaces.

Semaphore signals are rare in China but this superb set guards the southern approach to Liu Shu, the first crossing-point on the Nancha to Yichun line. Here a QJ storms south from Yichun in order to attack the steep climb which lies ahead.

BELOW: A QJ-hauled passenger train from Nancha to Yichun rolls gently down the bank towards Liu Shu having topped the climb from Nancha. Notice that the banking-engine is still attached; this will be

uncoupled when the train reaches Liu Shu.
ABOVE: The walk between Nancha and Liu Shu is
both beautiful and invigorating, especially in winter

when the blue sky, golden sunlight, snowy bracken-
clad landscape, magical exhaust effects and
colourfully-decorated locomotives make for the very
finest in lineside photography.

It was believed that China would retain steam traction well into the 21st century but, as
the country liberalises and moves away from rigid centralised government, the railway
bureaux with their newly formed autonomy have opted for more modern forms of
traction. There has been a nationwide shift away from steam, reminiscent of the one
which occurred in Britain between 1954 and 1968, when almost 20,000 steam
locomotives were scrapped. As was the case in Britain, it seems certain that relatively
new locomotives will go to the scrapyard prematurely, and that by the early years of the
new century the last great steam nation will have conformed to world practice, bringing
to a conclusion a 200-year dynasty, which began when Richard Trevithick's first
locomotive crawled from a South Wales ironworks in 1804.

Locomotive remains at Manzhouli on the Chinese-Russian border. The top picture was made at Zalainuei on 2nd February 1987, and features fragments of a JF 2-8-2 which resembles a Henry Moore sculpture. The picture below which also features a JF, was taken at the same location seven years later on 15th January 1994. These pictures illustrate the national trend to replace the older JFs, sturdy and strong as they are, either with diesels or more modern SY 2-8-2s.

ABOVE: An SY 2-8-2 deep in the huge open-cast pit at Zalainuei. The tracks are slewed as the workings extend across the landscape, spoil and coal being carried out by rail.

These scenes come from the now-closed forestry system at Lanxiang. The 762mm-gauge engines were of a standard design, although Lanxiang's engines had been built in Poland as well as China, where some had come from the Forest Machinery Company's works in Harbin. The system had over 100 route-miles of track and included a regular passenger service for forestry workers. The line's purpose was to bring logs from the forest to the huge sawmill at Lanxiang from which they were transferred by main-line railway to Harbin some three hundred kilometres to the south. Following the arrival at Lanxiang of Canadian 'experts' the logging operations were taken over by heavy trucking. Fortunately, many other steam worked forestry systems survive in China, especially in Heilongjiang Province.

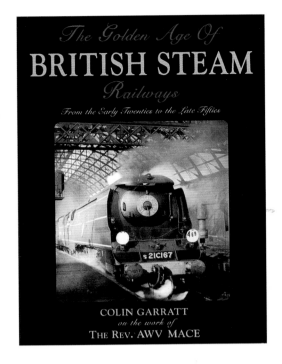

THE GOLDEN AGE OF

BRITISH STEAM

Railways

From the Early Twenties to the Late Fifties

COLIN GARRATT
on the work of
THE REV. AWV MACE

MILEPOST

This book has been produced in conjunction with Milepost 92½, which comprises a team of talented individuals led by Colin Garratt, specialising in audio-visual production, photographic services and a picture library for the Railway Industry.

For further information on Milepost 92½'s activities, please contact:

Milepost 92½,
Newton Harcourt,
Leicestershire,
LE8 9FH,
England.

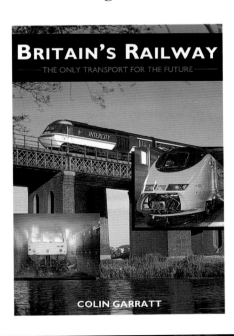